CATS

Anna Pollard

TREASURE
PRESS

CONTENTS

Like all Longhairs, this tabby-and-white has a long silky coat with a ruff around its neck, small tufted ears, and large appealing eyes.

INTRODUCTION

There was once a time when sinuous long-legged cats with jewels dangling from the frail corners of their ears were worshipped in temples dedicated to the mistress of love.

There was also a time when cats were seen either as witches' familiars or as full-blown witches in disguise – and greatly feared as a result.

But whether regarded by man as goddess or devil, friend or foe, adored pet or obscure threat, cats themselves have remained essentially unchanged and today are as tough and as sure of their place as they were in their days as sacred beings.

Compared to dogs, goats, even pigs, cats are new arrivals when it comes to relationships with man. It was the ancient Egyptians who, around 2000 BC, first gave the cat house-room, and the animal that moved in was a large tabby with reddish ears and a friendly disposition. This was the African wildcat, *Felis libyca*.

Unlike its European cousin, the African tabby is spectacularly easy to tame. It also, like all small cats, eats rats and mice, and since the wealth of Egypt came from her great grain stores, it is easy to see how a working partnership between man and cat grew up.

Mice would pour into a granary, a cat would follow, and the astute farmer – far from chasing the cat away – would encourage it with milk and titbits. He might even adopt a family of orphaned kittens and bring them up by hand; the result would be a group of 'wild' cats so tame that they would seek out a human's presence rather than avoid it. In this way, both the farmer and his family discovered the pleasures – as well as the convenience – of having a cat around the place;

Trees provide a resting-place safe from earth-bound enemies, such as dogs, and are a vantage point for the cats' own predatory instincts. They also provide useful scratching posts.

and kittens, of course, were every bit as charming then as they are now.

But the ancient Egyptians were not only the first people to domesticate the cat; they were also the first to fall completely under its spell. Its liking for the night, its eyes that glowed in the dark, its fertility and its grace all pointed to one thing: the cat was a sacred animal ruled by the moon and the love-goddess Pasht, who protected the sun from harm during its nightly absence from the sky. All over Egypt, be-jewelled cats were given free run through Pasht's temples and were adored by worshippers. (A faint memory of that worship lingers on in our own word Puss, based on the goddess's name.) Domestic mousers did almost as well in Egypt as the sacred cats. If one died, its owners shaved off their eyebrows in mourning, bought costly spices for embalming their pet's body, and finally buried the tiny cat mummy with great ceremony. To kill a cat deliberately was an appalling crime, punished by death.

It was the Romans who started the once-wild African cat on its journey north into Europe. To begin with, cats were looked on mainly as rather exotic pets, since most households of the Roman empire already had an excellent ratter in the shape of a tame weasel. But in the end, the cats forced the weasels out, mated with local wild felines and increased their numbers to the point where a domestic cat was an established and highly desirable part of any homestead. So much so that about AD 1000, a Welsh prince, Howel Dda, ordered that any cat-killer should pay a fine of as much grain as would cover the corpse held up by its tail (it made a sizeable mound). European house-cats were settling down to a future that looked as rosy as their Egyptian past had been glorious. It was a future that never came true.

In the late 1400s, Pope Innocent VIII officially decreed that witches' cats should be burnt in the same flames as the witches themselves. Something had changed with man's attitude to cats. Why? Part of the answer lies in the cat's ancient links with Egypt and the moon. The ancient Egyptians were pagans, and the moon was a symbol of the pre-Christian religions of Europe that the medieval church was desperately trying to stamp out. Cats, and especially black cats, were dubbed creatures of Satan, and suffered accordingly.

But would the Satan idea have caught on if cats had not had a curious power of turning otherwise normal people into frantic cat-haters? Probably not. The very things that made the Egyptians give such special love to their pets – the glowing eyes, the lithe movements, the independence mixed with gracious friendliness – all combined to bring Europe out in a rash of official cat-hatred. The occasional story of cat-allergies would have merely driven the fears deeper: here was proof, observers told each other, that cats really were fiends in furry guise.

So, for years, cats were tortured and burnt with the blessing of every authority, from the Church downwards. Even when that blessing lapsed, the idea that a cat was a false-hearted, worthless and generally inferior animal persisted for many years. However, there were some exceptions to this rule, along with some exceptional owners.

During the war-torn 1600s, the great French philosopher Montaigne found time to observe his pet and to note down one of the most profound thoughts about cats ever recorded. 'When I play with my cat,' he wrote, 'who knows whether she does not amuse herself more with me than I do with her?'

One century later, we have the King of France himself, Louis XV, delivering a stinging rebuke to his courtiers. They had poured perfume over his pet white Persian. (Longhaired cats had first been imported into Europe in the 1600s.)

However, better days for cats were not too far off. As the eighteenth century gave way to the nineteenth, people slowly started to become more humane, more scientifically aware and more interested in animals. Perhaps the final seal of approval was set on catdom when a British artist, Harrison Weir, mounted the first-ever cat show at the Crystal Palace in 1871. The Crystal Palace might not have been a temple of Pasht, but it was the next best thing. 'There they lay in their different pens,' Weir recalled, 'reclining on crimson cushions, making no sound save now and then a homely purring, as from time to time they lapped the nice new milk provided for them . . .' And, meanwhile, the public thronged round, admiring the black cats, white cats, tabbies and tortoise-shells just as they do at a Cat Fancy show today.

Weir, Montaigne and all history's other cat-lovers would have been delighted and dazed if they could have visited a modern cat show. So many different cats, all at the peak of condition and contentment; so many different varieties, many of them unknown before this century: the Siamese arrived in the west somewhere in the 1880s; the Burmese is much newer. The sparkling Chinchilla with its dark-rimmed eyes has been around for a long while but its pink-shaded cousin, the Cameo, is a recent arrival. And what about the Colour-point, the Chestnut Brown Foreign, the curly-coated Rex? The Rex, in particular, continues to raise eyebrows even now.

Weir and the others would have felt on surer ground on meeting the exhibitors. Throughout all time, cat-lovers have spoken the same basic language, whether they're rich or poor, young or old, owners of prize Persians or hosts to a mob of visiting moggies.

Some cat fanciers adopt a mask of detachment, but others don't bother; their attention is riveted on their pets; they croon to them, encourage them, love them. 'Oh, Pussy,' they say. 'Oh, Pussy!' Somewhere the goddess smiles. And everything between cat and man is marvellous.

Cats have developed into a variety of different types, each with distinctive features. Opposite are two cats with pedigrees – and one mongrel. But it is obvious that the odd-cat-out is not the young cream Persian (*top left*). Everything about it – neat ears, short nose, luxurious coat and enormous eyes – has been produced by many generations of careful breeding.

The pure-bred Abyssinian (*top right*) also has papers to prove its pedigree. According to some experts, the breed is thousands of years old. There are two varieties of Abyssinian, brown and red. The red one is sometimes called Sorrel while brown Abyssinians are often called 'bunny-colored'. This is because their coat is a similar color to that of a wild rabbit. In both rabbit and cat, each hair is ticked – that is, banded with a darker shade.

The tabby enjoying the Sardinian sunshine (*below right*) is a mixture of breeds. An ancestor similar to the Abyssinian gave it those slanting eyes and large ears. But the rest of it is a legacy from thousands of domestic European cats.

NINE LIVES

Nine lives? Well, perhaps; but it's not just luck that keeps cats out of trouble. It is their own superb ability to fit in with their surroundings, whatever these may be. They are delighted to be someone's pet – and, like the young tabby-and-white opposite, they don't mind being kept waiting. If, though, no one wants them, they will fend for themselves. The alley cats shown below are completely self-sufficient, and they like it that way. They live by hunting, scavenging and occasionally scrounging titbits.

The hunter

Cats are natural hunters. The most cosseted of indoor pets will chase a piece of string, a ball, or a toy mouse; the champion of a hundred shows will take to the woods in search of game, given half a chance. And ordinary cats, like the one shown on the left, will spend many hours practising all the skills of the chase: running, jumping, climbing, stalking. Training starts early: the kitten pouncing on its mother's tail is preparing for the day when it will pounce on something it is going to eat. And, as its strength grows, it will begin to hunt in earnest.

Unlike many of today's pedigree dogs, even the most highly bred of modern cats retains all the aids to hunting efficiency that kept its wild ancestors alive. Its supple spine gives it tremendous sprinting and leaping abilities; its large eyes and ears catch every tell-tale sign of its prey's whereabouts. Its claws are an essential part of its climbing equipment, and are also deadly weapons in their own right. And its tail helps it to balance. (The tailless Manx seems to manage very well without a built-in balancing pole; but its lack is compensated for by extra-long hind legs.) Unless matched against a true expert like a squirrel, cats are brilliant climbers – as long as they keep going upwards. It is when they come down that they can start to have problems, as all fire brigades and embarrassed cat-owners know. Cats can in fact jump down from considerable heights and survive; their legendary ability to land on their feet is another item in their survival kit. But there is a limit to what even the most daredevil cat can do without crossing another of those nine lives off its total.

When it comes to smelling things out, cats are not in the dog class. But the tortoiseshell-and-white (*right*) can manage quite happily with what her nose is telling her. The vast majority of tortoiseshells are female; the very rare males are always infertile. Tortoiseshell-and-whites are also called Calico cats.

All farmyards are a cat's idea of heaven; for the ginger on the opposite page, they are its place of work as well. Most modern farmers, like the ancient Egyptians centuries ago, keep a cat to catch rats and mice and such cats happily earn their keep.

Coming down? In fact, the tree-climber below is not in such difficulties as it looks. Its next move it to get all its legs onto one bough and then descend . . . backwards.

Fat cats

A bowl of milk does not go far when shared between three slim cats that want to grow fatter. Oddly enough, some cats do not like milk at all, although most love cream. One of the cats shown here looks as though it has been crowded out and, to ensure fair shares all round, it makes sense to give each cat in a household its individual bowl.

A cat's main food is meat. Butcher's meat or canned meat; meat chopped up in the kitchen; meat caught and eaten in the garden: it is all the same to hungry cats like the two shown below. If they do not get their dish filled, they will certainly be off to find an alternative source of supply.

As a side-line, cats have also been known to like, among other things: cheese, ice-cream, butter (especially melted butter), fish paste, cocktail biscuits, currant buns, cabbage, cornflakes, and raw egg yolk. Every cat, in short, has its own

very special idea of what makes an extra-good treat (see also Caring for Your Cat, on page 40). Not all cats like fish. But every single one – whether it is a meat-eater, a fish-fancier or a food faddist that is hooked on one single brand of canned cat-food – enjoys chewing grass. It helps the digestion.

During the first month of its life, a kitten lives on its mother's milk. Like the tiny Siamese kittens below, it will spend most of its time sleeping or suckling. Each kitten has its 'own' teat, and is particular about feeding from that one and that one only. To make the mother's milk come down, the kitten paddles away at the mother's belly as it feeds. This paddling action will remain with a cat for life. Whenever, for example, it is sitting on a friendly lap, it will sink all its claws into the owner's knees in a spirit of pure contentment.

Kittens start experimenting with solid food when they are about four weeks old; by this time, most of their milk teeth have broken through. (They are born blind and toothless.) Weaning ends at about seven weeks.

Grooming

A clean cat is an efficient cat. Lank fur does not keep the cold out; dirty fur smells and interferes with the cat's own sense of scent. No cat, of course, reasons it out like this, but, at the same time, no cat is happy after a meal until it has washed itself thoroughly. Washing also serves a useful social purpose. A cat which is perplexed or put out will often give itself a token lick; this is the feline equivalent of scratching one's nose or taking an unwanted sip of coffee.

Kittens learn to groom themselves by copying their mother's example. With practice, they soon find out that they can reach every single part of themselves, either with the tongue or with a well-licked paw. The paw technique is used for grooming the face and behind the ears; the ginger on the left is just reaching the behind-the-ears stage.

CAT PARADE

Cats vary in their size and there are a huge array of colors. But, unlike dogs, they have only one basic shape. Within the basic cat framework, however, there are some subtle differences of shape that are very important to breeders. If the Longhaired cat opposite had the big ears, slender legs and ultra-long tail of the Siamese below, its owner would despair. In the same way, a chunky Siamese would never score in the show-ring, and a Domestic Shorthaired cat with a slim, Siamese-type body would also lose marks. The following pages explore some of the variations on this basic theme and show what the dividing lines are.

Variations on a theme...

Enter the Domestic Shorthair – also known as the American Shorthair, British Shorthair or European Shorthair. Whatever name it goes by, it remains one of the three main types of cat that breeders aim to produce. The black-and-white posing on a tree-stump (*opposite*) shows off the type's main features: sleek and well-proportioned, it has neat ears, a powerful neck and chest, cobby feet and smooth, short fur.

The tabby (*below*) demonstrates another important feature of the breed: full, plump cheeks. So does the British Blue (*left*), one of the best known of all the Shorthaired breeds.

'I have a Gumbie Cat in mind, her name
    is Jennyanydots;
Her equal would be hard to find, she likes
    the warm and sunny spots . . . '
T. S. Eliot might have been writing about the
tabby Domestic Shorthair shown below, which
has chosen a sun-baked corner in which to
meditate. At the same time, it shows off the
classic 'bracelets' on front and hind legs that
all high-class tabbies must have.

No pedigrees, perhaps, for the ginger and the
black-and-white shown on the opposite page.
But Ginger – who is really a pale red tabby –
carries an 'M' on its forehead in true tabby style,
while its companion also has a neatly marked
face. A good bi-color isn't just any black, red,
blue or cream cat splashed with white; at least
a third of the coat has to be white, and
maybe more.

The beautifully marked, young, silver tabby (*far left*) is almost of prize-winning standard. It has hazel eyes, a perfect 'M' on the forehead and a double necklace (known by cat-fanciers as the 'Lord Mayor's Chains') across the chest. Only the white patch on its front could bar it from winning rosettes. Quite often, cat shows have a section for the prettiest pet, as opposed to the most perfect breed specimen; it would stand a chance of winning on this front too.

Namesakes (*below*): A bi-colored cat amongst the catkins. The idea of cats and catkins going together occurs in France as well: the French for catkin is *chaton*, or kitten.

At home on the farm: a domestic tabby (*left*) in domestic surroundings. Farm cats like this one often live almost entirely off the creatures they manage to catch.

Foreign Shorthaired

Somewhere in these four cats' ancestry is a Siamese. The white cat (*below*) is in fact a Siamese without the distinctive dark points; the dark brown cat (*right*) derives from a now-distant mating between a Siamese and a black Longhair, while its kitten shows yet another genetic influence. Its father was a tabby-point Siamese (also called Lynx Point). An adult tabby-point is shown opposite.
All four are members of the second of the three big cat groups recognized by breeders: the Foreign Shorthairs. The official name of the white one is the Foreign White, and the striped kitten's mother is a Chestnut Brown Foreign (sometimes called a Havana).

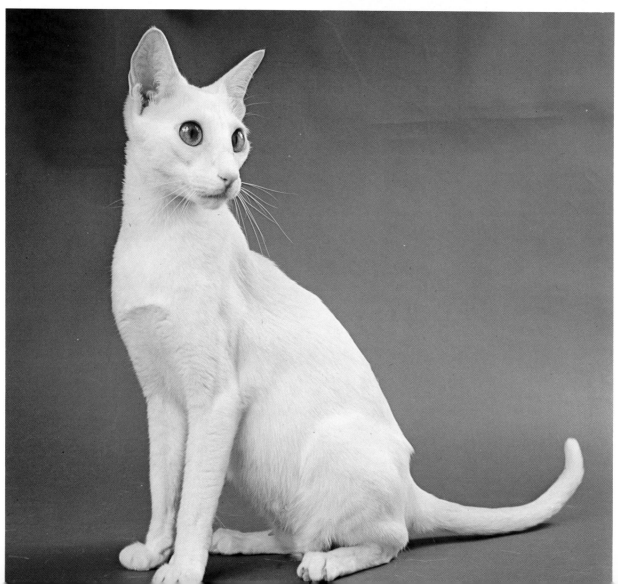

No cat fanciers have so far recognized a breed called the Red Tabby Foreign. If they did, however, the young ginger cat below could be a founder-member. It has all the hall-marks of the Foreign type: large ears, wedge-shaped face, slim neck, long legs, oval feet and a whiplash tail. Its eyes are of the classic Foreign almond shape – and if its coat is too pale by Domestic Shorthair standards, that can be put right for its descendants by a careful breeding program. Prominent whisker-pads complete the picture.

While the Siamese in all its variety of points – seal, blue, chocolate, lilac (frost), red, tabby and tortoiseshell – is easily the best known of all the Foreign Shorthairs, there are others that are nearly as popular. The Blue Burmese (*below*) and its brown cousin between them share a particularly devoted following, especially among cat-lovers who find the Siamese too noisy for comfort.

The Abyssinian, whether 'bunny-colored' or red, also gets a good share of attention, and so does the Russian Blue (picture on page 47).

But the Chestnut Brown Foreign is rare, while another self-color, the Lavender, is not yet recognized everywhere.

Not all Foreign cats have short, smooth coats. The Balinese (again, not recognized everywhere) is a Siamese with long fur and the Rex has a highly distinctive curly coat. There are two strains of Rex, the Cornish and the Devon; named after their counties of origin in England. It is now possible to breed them marked in the Siamese pattern. Since their fur is thin, Rex cats tend to feel the cold.

Longhaired

Rarest of the rare: a Longhaired silver tabby. A perfect specimen is extremely hard to find or breed. Most Longhairs have their coats carefully brushed upwards and outwards before going on the show bench, but the silver tabbies are an exception. The owner of this one has smoothed the fur down so that the fine tabby pencillings can be seen. Both ruff and tail, though, are as fluffy as any lover of Longhaired cats could wish.

The Longhairs – or Persians, as they are often called – make up the third big group of pedigree cats. (Non-pedigree cats, of course, can also have long hair, and many do.) Apart from its coat, a good Longhair differs from cats in the other groups in several ways. Nose, legs and tail are shorter; the ears are smaller; the face is broader. The body is strong and solid without being ungainly. The eyes are very large and round – a feature that gives the Longhairs the appealing expression they are famed for (demonstrated opposite).

In general, the Longhaired breeds follow the same color patterns as the Domestic Shorthairs. Black Longhairs are sought-after but rare.

A good Longhaired white is everyone's idea of a perfect cat, and reds and red tabbies (*left*) have their own type of splendor, even when young. The Longhaired tortoiseshell-and-white (*below*) is an all-female breed.

Cats' eyes

Five pairs of eyes: amber, blue, yellow and – on the opposite page – a mixture. Among the Longhaired aristocrats of the cat world, only the silver tabby and the white Chinchilla are allowed to have eyes of the color we usually associate with cats: green.

The standard eye color for the blue-cream cat (*below left*) is copper or orange; that for the Colorpoint (*below right*) is Siamese-style blue. Blue Persians (*bottom left*) and Smokes (*bottom right*) must also have deep orange or copper-colored eyes.

The blue-and-yellow stare of the white cat opposite makes it a breed all on its own: the Odd-eyed White. The classic colors for Whites are either blue or orange; but blue-eyed Whites (which are only one stage short of being albinos) are often deaf. This does not apply, of course, to the Colourpoint – or to any of the blue-eyed Foreign Shorthairs. The Colorpoint, or Himalayan, is not, in fact, a Longhaired Siamese but a true Longhair that has been bred with Siamese markings. The Balinese – which really *is* a Siamese with long fur – has slimmer legs, larger ears, and a much longer tail.

The cat's reputation for uncanniness owes a lot to the way its eyes glow in the dark. The blue Persian (*bottom left*) demonstrates how this mysterious glow is produced. The photographer's light is shining straight into the cat's eyes, and is being reflected back through the pupils. It is this built-in reflecting mechanism that helps a cat to see well in the dark. It gets a 'double dose' of whatever light there is. But no cat can see in total darkness.

A red tabby and a Birman: the Birman is one
of the most unusual of the Longhairs. At first
sight, it looks like a Colorpoint, but the white
paws are a giveaway. All Birmans have them.

CARING FOR YOUR CAT

FEEDING

Cats are natural meat eaters. Suitable foods include raw beef, cooked lamb, cooked tripe, cooked *and boned* rabbit, chicken, white fish. Raw liver can be given in moderation; too much can cause diarrhea. Many canned cat foods are very good but do not rely on these to the exclusion of other foods.

Cats also need to chew grass. If your cat has no access to a garden, grow some grass in a pot. Some cats like milk; others don't.

Throw away left-over food after each meal – but make sure that a bowl of fresh water is available at all times. This is doubly important if your cat eats dried food.

Adult cats need one good meal a day, given in the evening. Weaned kittens need four small meals, with a fair quantity of milk-based foods.

CAT MANAGEMENT

All cats need a warm, draught-free place to sleep. If you do not provide one, your pet will choose its own: your bed, sofa, or best armchair. (Cats should not be allowed to sleep on beds.) All pet shops stock sleeping baskets for cats, but a good cat bed can be made out of a cardboard box. Line it with newspaper or an old blanket.

Many cat-owners install a hinged cat-door, enabling their cats to roam outside at will. If you do not, make sure to give your cat a tray in which it can relieve itself. A plastic washing-up bowl will do: half-fill it with earth or cat litter and stand it on a newspaper. Change the litter every day, washing the bowl out thoroughly.

Cats which go out should be equipped with a collar and name tag. The collar *must* have an elastic insert; this allows the cat to slip out of it easily if it gets caught on a tree. A collar made of solid material could strangle its wearer.

Cats need to sharpen their claws frequently. A cat which spends all its time indoors should be given a scratching post, available from pet shops. Otherwise, it will sharpen its claws on the furniture.

HANDLING

To pick up a cat, put one hand under its chest and the other under its back legs. Do not pick it up by the nape of the neck – and do not allow children to pull a cat about. It is not only miserable for the cat; it could be dangerous for the child.

Sick cats can be restrained from scratching if they are gently swaddled in a sheet or towel. The cat's head, of course, should stick out.

DISCIPLINE

If a cat does anything that must be discouraged, shake your finger in front of its nose and say 'No!' loudly. Repeat – in as deep a voice as possible – when the offence is about to recur. Do not try smacking; where cats are concerned, corporal punishment just does not work. A more practical aid is oil of citronella, available from a pharmacy. Cats hate the smell, so sprinkling some on a disputed bit of territory or furniture should end the problem overnight. (Be warned, though: it has a very strong smell indeed. A couple of drops will be all that is needed.)

GROOMING

Regular grooming is important. Longhaired cats should be groomed once a day (use a bristle brush and steel comb); Shorthairs need less frequent attention. Even these, however, should be groomed at least once a week.

If a cat is not groomed often enough, the loose hair it licks off will accumulate in its intestines and form a blockage. This particularly applies during its twice-yearly moult.

If your cat's fur becomes badly matted, carefully cut the mat out with scissors.

VACATIONS

Over very short periods, you can leave your cat at home – as long as a really reliable neighbor agrees to visit twice a day, feed it, and change its litter.

A cat in a strange house should be kept in for at least three days after arrival, although it is a good idea to walk it round the garden on a lead morning and evening.

NEUTERING AND SPAYING

Cats that are not needed for breeding purposes

should be neutered (castrated) or spayed by a vet. A spayed female will not be able to have kittens; a neutered male, unlike a tom, will not spray, fight for females or yowl. Careful attention to diet will stop a neutered male putting on weight.

BREEDING
Unspayed females – called 'queens' – are able to bear kittens from the age of eight months onwards. They come into season at least twice a year, and show it by rolling on the ground, displaying extra affection, and howling. They also do their best to get out: if they do, owners will be presented with a litter of mongrel kittens 63 days later.

If you want to breed from your cat, choose a mate well in advance and take the queen to the tom as soon as she comes into season. She should not be mated until she is a year old, and she should not have more than two litters a year.

A pregnant queen can lead her normal life. But give her extra food (especially milky dishes) when she demands it. Towards the end of her pregnancy, her appetite will be much bigger than usual, and she will also need extra food while she is feeding her kittens.

Shortly before the kittens are due, line a stout cardboard box with newspaper and place it in a warm, quiet spot out of draughts and strong light. Make sure the cat knows where it is. Each kitten is born in a transparent sac, which the queen breaks. She also nips through the umbilical cord, and washes the kitten thoroughly. The kitten will then want to suckle.

Do not interfere with the birth process; do, though, keep an eye on how the cat is getting on. If there are any signs of real trouble, send for the veterinary surgeon.

Kittens are born blind and toothless. Their mother will do all the rearing and training necessary, but an owner can start helping to wean the kittens from about three weeks onwards, using baby foods. Their first meat meal (cooked, boned and mashed) comes when they are about five weeks old.

Although they will be fully weaned seven or eight weeks after birth, they should not be separated from their mother until they are ten weeks old at least.

ILLNESSES
The most frightening disease that can strike a cat is Feline Infectious Enteritis. Appallingly contagious, it is also a killer. However, vaccination gives near-complete immunity, so have your cat vaccinated as soon as you get it. (If buying a kitten, ask if this has been done already.) Do not forget the booster-shots, either; your veterinary surgeon will tell you when the next one is due.

Other cat illnesses include anemia, bronchitis, colds, and cat 'flu (also called pneumonitis, and potentially fatal).

A sick cat is unmistakable. It is uninterested in food or exercise. Sometimes its nose or eyes run; sometimes its 'haws' (the third eyelid at the inside corner of each eye) may show. Its fur goes lank, and it may suffer from vomiting or diarrhea. It often hunches up in a corner and refuses to leave it.

If you notice some or all of these symptoms, call in the vet immediately. It may be nothing serious – but if it turns out to be enteritis, every minute counts.

A cat may pick up fleas or lice. These can be treated with an insecticide specifically intended for pets. Read the label to check that cats are included, and follow the maker's instructions carefully. Suspect ear mites (canker) if the cat scratches its ears a great deal, and have the cat treated.

A flea-ridden cat may end up with a bad case of tapeworm. Segments of tapeworm – like small grains of rice – are likely to be visible under the cat's tail, in its motions, and in its bed or basket. In addition, the cat may have a huge appetite and yet look out of condition. Kittens are particularly susceptible to another internal parasite, the round worm. When passed in the kitten's movements, it looks like a thin piece (or pieces) of string.

After touching a cat that is out-of-sorts in any way, be particularly careful to wash your hands thoroughly. Anyone nursing a sick cat should wear an overall.

CATS WITH A PAST

All cats have a past. Indeed, some manage to build up more pasts than one: owners frequently find out that their faithful, home-loving pet has been leading a double life as someone else's faithful pet during the daylight hours. But only the Abyssinian (*opposite*) can boast of an ancestral past that – perhaps – goes right back to the sacred cats of ancient Egypt. According to some experts, it was the Abyssinian's forefathers that were worshipped in the temples of the goddess Pasht. True or false, no one is quite sure – just as no one is really quite sure of the origins of the Birman (*below*). One legend says they are descended from a band of sacred cats that watched over the temples of Burma, and that their leader was the reincarnation of a saintly abbot. The golden tinge in their fur, the legend goes on, is a reflection of the halo that shone round the abbot's head.

No cats have had a past quite so dramatic, so lurid, or so misunderstood as the plain black mouser. The black cat of today (*opposite*) still manages to give us a faint feeling of awe; but that is nothing compared to the emotions it aroused in our ancestors. In the Middle Ages, and for long afterwards, black cats were regarded with complete mistrust. They were – so people believed – creatures of Satan, witches in disguise, assistants to all those who practised the black arts. No pleased reception greeted the friendly black cat that tried to cross anyone's path: at the height of Europe's anti-cat mania, it would have been fortunate to escape with its life.

Even when the worst excesses of cat hatred had died down, black cats went on being associated with witches, spells, and magic generally. Amateur spell casters thought that black cats controlled the wind and the tides; amateur physicians swore that their fur had curative properties. And, although these beliefs have been shattered by science and common sense, two last remnants of superstition still cling. In Britain a black cat is thought to bring good luck, especially when it crosses your path. In the United States the occurrence is still reckoned to be a bad omen.

Although black cats were particularly linked with witches in the past, a witch's cat did not have to be black. 'Thrice the brinded cat hath mewed,' says one of the hags in Shakespeare's *Macbeth* – and she could have been referring to the brinded (or brindled) tabby below. A grey cat, in fact, turns up on the very first page of the play: 'I come, Graymalkin!' screams the witch, talking to her unseen familiar. Grimalkin was once a common name for an old female cat – or a spiteful old lady.

When Siamese cats first appeared in the west in the 1880s, they were instantly dubbed the 'Royal Cats of Siam'. The Siamese below certainly has a regal air – but there is more to the 'royal cat' story than mere looks. According to legend, the cats were pets of the royal princesses of Siam. When the girls went bathing, the cats went too – but not to swim. Their job was to guard their mistresses' jewellery. Each princess would slide her rings on to a cat's tail; the cat would wrap its laden tail tightly round its legs; and the rings were safe until the princess came back.

All went well until one of the cats, seeing its mistress appear, jumped up too quickly. All the rings slid off into the pool and were lost for ever. So, next time, the girls took precautions: each one slid her rings on to her cat's tail . . . and tied a firm knot in the end. Every day, the cats acted as living jewellery stands and, every day, the knots were untied at the end of the swim and the rings removed. But, with so much knotting and untying, a kink began to appear in the cats' tails, and has stayed there ever since. Two other breeds that come with legends attached are the Manx and the Russian Blue. The Manx, they say, first arrived on the Isle of Man during the wreck of the Spanish Armada. Another story says that Noah, in his hurry, shut the door of the Ark on the Manx's once-long tail.

The Russian Blue (*below left*) is thought by some to have originated in the Russian port of Archangel. The Russian Blue's Abyssinian companion (*below right*) is clearly practising for the role of another well-known cat in a story: the Cheshire variety, created by Lewis Carroll.

MOODS

Like people, cats have moods. And,
unlike people, they are incapable of
hiding them. A happy cat can deafen
you with its purring; a disapproving
one can deliver a snub that makes its
owners cringe. You cannot mistake a
cross cat, either, or a worried cat, or a
wheedling cat, or a suspicious cat like
the tabby opposite. By half-closing
their eyes, cats can produce the
appearance of the most charming
smile, but their sense of humor,
though subtle, is one-sided.
They hate being laughed at!

Curious cats

'Curiosity killed the cat', says the proverb. But this same curiosity is, in fact, one of the most important items in a cat's survival kit. The black-and-white below heard something that startled it: what it will do next depends on what it heard. If a dog barked, it will run; if a bird chirruped, it will give chase. Either way, it needs to know – so, with muscles tensed, it stares in the direction of the noise. A cat in strange surroundings will behave in the same keyed-up way: it will explore, poke into corners, investigate potential obstacles and danger spots. Only when it has checked up on everything around can it relax. Nothing ever escapes an alert cat's notice.

Dignified, self-contained and drowsy, this
Domestic Shorthair does not want to be
disturbed under any circumstances. It
epitomizes the serene independence that
cats are famous for.

Taking it easy

Cats often seem to divide their time between quivering alertness and deep, dead-to-the-world sleep. While they all have an immense talent for relaxing, a sleeping cat is not really as comatose as it looks. It may yawn (*opposite below*), and tuck in its paws and close its eyes (*left*). But it will only be drowsing – or cat-napping. The cat snoozing on a flight of steps (*left*) is beginning to let itself go. If not disturbed, its nose will droop lower, its muscles will relax and it will start to dream. A dreaming cat is unmistakable: it twitches, works its paws, yammers gently to itself and behaves not unlike a dreaming human. Basking in the sun (*below*) is a favorite relaxation.

Cats have a way of expressing their enjoyment of what can properly be called creature comforts. The head down, roly-poly posture seen overleaf is actually a greeting gesture, too. (Cats using this form of greeting will often turn near-complete somersaults.) It has its origins in the fact that an animal lying with its stomach exposed is highly vulnerable to attack. But an aggressor of the same species finds that its aggression is cut off at source when the opponent deliberately falls into the stomach-bared, 'I give up', position. Domestic cats (and many dogs) do it to show complete trust and affection.

Cat conversation

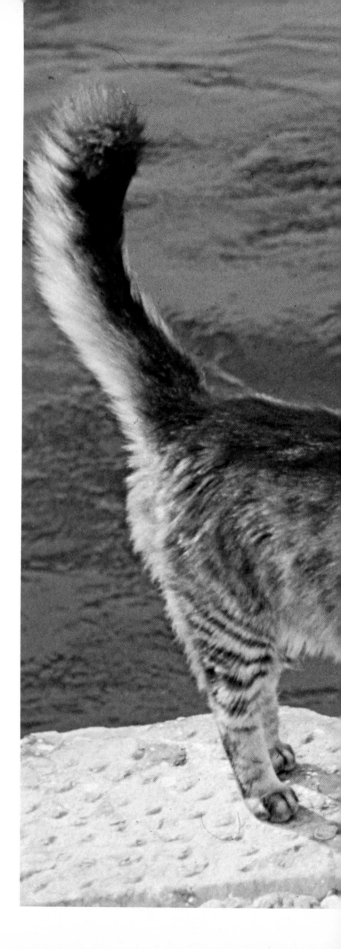

The tabbies on the right are deep in silent communication. What they are saying is, of course, their secret; but, judging by the slightly tense posture of the cat standing up, it is not all that pleasant. Cats use their whole bodies to talk with, and, in cat-to-cat conversation, body language is usually enough. An angrily swishing tail is only one sign of feline emotion, and an obvious one. Others are: expanded pupils – excitement or rage; backward-pointing ears – fear; flattened ears – part of the battle posture; tail carried straight up, with tip hanging over – contentment; blinking – also contentment.
An interested, friendly cat has its ears pricked forward, its eyes wide open, and its muscles relaxed. An angry cat, on the other hand, presses its ears back, hunches up, ruffles its fur and walks on legs as stiff as any Wild West gun-fighter.
A fighting cat also spits, snarls, growls and hisses at its opponent. But cats reserve most of their vocal conversation for humans. As all owners know, they can produce a wide variety of mews, a bird-like chirp, a howl, a squeak and a purr that ranges from a subdued mutter to a full-throated, room-filling rumble. Oddly enough, the mechanics of purring baffle scientists.

Self–expression

Tigers are big cats. And cats can behave like little tigers. Their instincts are to run, chase, pounce, kill. The tabby opposite is not an image from a nightmare but a cat at the height of aggression. This is what all kittens' games lead up to; this is what the dreamer on the hearthrug is really dreaming of.
Even the most devoted cat-lover has the odd qualm when his pet kills birds, plays with mice and demonstrates the ruthlessness of nature. From our angle, it looks awful, and – again from our angle – it is. But the cat sees things differently: it is what it is and cannot pretend to be otherwise.
Part of the squeamish owner's trouble stems from an over-rational approach: 'I feed Blackie twice daily, so why does he go and crunch up small birds?' In fact, Blackie will often eat his prey and then come racing in for his dinner: the hunt has stimulated his appetite better than the prospect of canned food could do. But the owner's real problem lies in not fully accepting the ambiguity of the cat's status in a domestic setting. It is both home-lover and jungle-dweller. We prize cats because they retain an air of wildness, and we delight in seeing them practise their ancestral skills on a catnip mouse. The corpses on the lawn are the price of that delight.
The cats below seem to be involved in an unusual occupation: the gang going 'out on the town' or on the prowl. As a concerted group occupation this is not typical, but it is reminiscent of other branches of the cat family such as lions.

Cat expressions can mean many different things: fear (*right*); anxiety (*below*); self-assertion (*opposite, below*); and the beginnings of aggression (*opposite, top right*). All kittens can look pathetic, but it takes a full grown blue Persian, with a long pedigree, to produce a compellingly powerful stare like the one shown opposite, top left.

The cat in the snow (*opposite, below*) is alert, self-assured, pleased with life in general and with the weather in particular. Although cats are well known for their love of warmth, many enjoy the snow as well, and plow fearlessly into drifts until they are chest deep. They are, of course, well protected against the cold by their coat.

INDEX

Italicized numbers refer to illustrations

FRONT COVER PHOTOGRAPH:
OCTOPUS GROUP/JOHN MOSS
BACK COVER PHOTOGRAPH:
OCTOPUS GROUP/ROBERT
ESTALL

This edition published in 1990 by
Treasure Press, Michelin House,
81 Fulham Road, London SW3 6RB

© 1979 Octopus Books Limited

ISBN 1 85051 488 7

Produced by Mandarin Offset
Printed in Hong Kong